Google Classroom:

The 2020 Ultimate Guide to Learning Everything about Google Classroom Management

By

James Gates

Table Of Contents

CHAPTER 01

INTRODUCTION TO GOOGLE CLASSROOM

Teaching is the oldest profession in the world. There have been various teaching methods used, primarily through humans teaching what they have observed and learned, transferring information and experience onto the next generation. Today, teaching is a complex subject that needs not only full devotion but knowledge on various technologies that provide interaction between teachers and students while online. If you need comprehensive, adaptable, easy-to-use, and no-strings-attached technology, then you might consider Google's free service, **Google Classroom**. A classroom perspective is always a place where teachers and students can collaborate, where an interactive mode of learning is available and where questions can be asked and answered. The classroom is also the space where teachers set assignments, project, or homework and this should be carried out in modern and flexible ways. Google Classroom is a free service created for schools that aims to facilitate the formation, dissemination, and scoring of work in a paperless environment.

Google Classroom's primary purpose is to facilitate the concept of allocating academics between educators and pupils. The platform is part of Google Apps for Education, an online application package for teachers and students to learn and collaborate online. Used primarily for institutional educational levels, this educational platform includes many popular Google apps such as Gmail, Calendar, Documents, Sheets, Slides, Google Drive, Forms, Jam board, Sites (Web builder), Meet, Groups, and Vault. Google Classroom is found only in the Google Education platform and it is considered an essential site in which teachers and students can correspond, schedule and submit homework, and send and receive feedback. Some of the key benefits of Google Classroom are that it is time-saving, easy-to-use, and has intuitive structural elements.

Google Classroom is first and foremost a Learning Management System Google introduced for tutors. It provides a central place for students to interact, ask queries, and set tasks. In the incredibly fast-paced AI world, Google Classroom provides online educational support for the digital pupils of today. Like many new apps, Google Classroom has a distinctive look and feel. Because the way your physical classroom is organized is as unique as you teach within it, Google Classroom offers a blank page for you to use as you see fit within the platform's features. Before students are added to Google Classroom you need to create virtual classes for your physical classes. As you use Google Classroom, it may be that no physical class is associated with your online one—for example, students enrolled in distance learning and significant school events may use Google Classroom without a physical class. First, you need to feel comfortable with all features provided in Google Classroom. As a teacher, the platform offers options students may not see and only allows tutors to change certain settings, such as what pupils can do in Google classroom. You can add students to the classroom, create notices and tasks, and upload course materials from this classroom perspective as a teacher. First, you need to create and organize your class.

Google Classroom uses Google Drive for assignment creating, uploading, and sharing. Google Docs, Sheets and Slides are used for writing, Gmail for email, and Google Calendar for scheduling. Students can be invited to join the class via a joining code or they can be routinely imported from your school's domain for easy student identification. Each class creates a separate folder in the user drive, where students can submit assignments for grading. Mobile apps are available for iOS and Android devices and allow users to take photos and add tasks. Students can also share files by using other apps and can access material offline. Teachers can administer each student's progress and after marking assignments they can return student work along with notes.

Modern applications from Google such as Gmail, Google Calendar, and Google Docs can become a beneficial combination to improve class working efficiency equivalent to that in the physical classroom. These collaborative platforms have modernized the way classes are conducted, work is collected, and how we store material online. For teachers and students, Google Classroom brings benefits of social platforms, learning platforms, virtual collaboration and paperless assignments to the classroom. Millions of tutors and students in various schools around the world use Google Classroom, making it one of the trendiest EDTECH tools available.

YOUR FIRST GOOGLE CLASS

Before we start creating our first class, there are some crucial things to understand.

1. Google Suite for Education a/c. To have access to this, the school or scholastic institution that hires you as a teacher must be part of the program. Students must also have the same account to access Google Classroom. In our instructions, we assume your given institute has obtained G Suite or has a GAFE account, as well as your students. In addition to Google Classroom, we encourage you to have access to all of Google's core apps such as Gmail, Google Calendar, Drive, Docs, Sheets, Slides, Forms, Jam-board,

sites, Meet, Groups, and Vault. This is so you can work with and provide an integrated communication and collaborative solution to students. A computer connected to the Internet is also required, running on Windows Vista or later, a Mac OS, or Chromebook.

2. Although Google Classroom is accessible from any web browser, Google Chrome is the recommended option as it is designed to work seamlessly with all Google apps. Therefore, some characteristics may be incompatible or may not work correctly in other web browsers. If you do not have Google Chrome installed on your computer, consider reviewing this with your school's IT department.

3. If it is your first time using Google Classroom you will notice the app asks if you want your role to be specified as teacher or student. Make sure you choose the teacher role correctly, otherwise, your account will be assigned as a student. You cannot create or manage classes unless you have a role as a teacher in Google Classroom. If your account is set up as a student account then you need to contact your IT department so they can edit your role to a teacher.

4. Another way to access Google Classroom is to use the App Launcher. If your IT department has enabled this feature, click on the waffle-shaped icon in the upper right corner of

another Google app, such as Gmail, to see if the Google Classroom icon exists. Below is an example of an app launcher.

5. After signing up for this free service your school should read the privacy and security notices thoroughly before agreeing to them.

After ensuring you have met the above prerequisites, you need to follow the below steps to create your classroom.

1. Once you select the role of teacher the next page indicates a plus sign in the upper right corner. This is where you will create your first class.

2. When you click on the plus sign it will ask you whether you want to create or join a class. Click **Create Class** to create your first class. As a teacher, you can also join another teacher's class as a student by clicking on the class and inputting the class code.

3. Next, you will see a dialogue box for you to provide class name, section, subject, and room. While class name is required, depending on your school policy, specific classes may already have section numbers you can add here. In Canada, many middle and high schools use these numbers for scheduling timetables, which is another option you can

add. Since students also see the section number a scheduled timetable is no longer applicable to them.

4. After selecting the **Create** button, you are shown a dialogue box or web page informing you about what's new in the classroom, prompting you to get ready for the school year. This includes seeing grades for all assignments on the grades page, test drive rubric, originality reports, and SIS grade synchronization, as well as allowing you to customize your stream.

LEARNING AND NAVIGATING GOOGLE CLASSROOM

Once these fields are filled out and the **Create** button is selected, you are taken to your new online classroom. Here, you can navigate the platform to learn all options available. Now your first class is created, you can see various options, banners, menus, sidebars, and content.

1. A banner image showing class name, section, subject, room number, and code is displayed at the top of Google Classroom. When students enter the classroom, the banner is the first thing they see so they can quickly identify which class they are attending. You can change the theme of the banner by clicking **Select theme**, where you can select themes according to your subject or choose other themes provided by Google. You can also select

Upload photo if you want to use a personalized image instead. Simply drag or select any photo from the computer to upload it as your new banner.

2. The menu allows teachers and students to switch between different parts of Google classroom. The menu has the following sub-sections:

    a. **Stream** is the page where announcements are made and scheduled. Teachers can post messages and respond to students.

    b. The **Classwork** tab is where you can assign tasks to your class by creating assignments and quizzes. You can provide material or reuse posts shared on the Stream by selecting **Create** and selecting from the links in the drop-down menu.

        i. In the **Assignment** menu of the drop-down list, you can assign assignments to students. You can input instructions or attach documents. You can assign the work to specific recipients, give total points, due date, and the topic. You can also create the Rubric (a heading, instruction, or rules) here.

        ii. You can create **Quizzes** by selecting it in the drop-down menu. On the page, provide a title and set of instructions (optional). Here you can also use Google Forms for creating your quiz assignment or you can attach files by clicking the **Add** button.

iii. The **Question** option contains a format to create questions using short answers and instruction (if any) you want to set. You can also attach files.

iv. You can create or add material to the **Material** section after clicking it from the drop-down menu and include similar information to the Question feature.

v. You can use **Topic** to organize classwork into modules or units. You can order work the way you would like your students to see.

vi. Classwork also includes **Google Calendar** and **Google Drive**. Selecting either will take you to the specific application where you can either schedule items in Google Calendar or upload assignments in Google Drive. Anything you do in either application will automatically synchronize across all your devices with Google applications.

c. The **People** tab of Google Classroom displays a list of all students enrolled in the class and teachers assigned to the class. You can invite students or provide them with the class code shown on the page. Similarly, you can enlist as many teachers as you like by typing their name or email on the page that appears after clicking the **Add** button. Teachers can also type student names or email addresses using the same method.

d. The **Grades** menu displays student marks.

3. On the left-hand side of Google Classroom, you will see a sidebar with **Settings**. These are your unique settings and where your profile and notification preferences can be adjusted to enhance usability.

4. On the upper right corner within the application, the setting icon is displayed. These are your class settings where you can change and manage class details, whether or not students are allowed to post and grading options.

CHAPTER 02

INVITING STUDENTS

After setting up your class in Google Classroom, you now want to invite your students to the class. You can invite as many students as you want through entering their email or you can give students a code that allows them to log into your classroom (which is an effortless way to go!).

Note: Students can unregister themselves from class, but once they unenroll their grades be removed.

It is the start of a new school term, your classrooms are configured and students are ready to enter and learn. Students can now simply sit at home rather than attend a physical classroom. Here is an online classroom where students must join the class from a computer or mobile device. Google Classroom is especially beneficial for classrooms when computers or mobile devices are readily available. Students can also often use this platform if it is readily accessible from their devices. If your school lends equipment to students on an individual basis then these applications may need to be installed. As a teacher, you will need to ensure your students install the required software and apps on their computer, tablet, or smart-phone and have them join Google Classroom.

INVITING STUDENTS BY EMAIL

To invite students or a group of students, you can use the Google Groups email alias. You do not need to be a group owner or member, but you should be able to see the members and see their email. If you cannot see this information, communicate it with your IT department to change the permissions or rights.

- Go to classroom.google.com

- Click the class you want to add to the student or group of students.

- Select the People tab and then the add symbol next to Students.

- Enter the email address of the student or group. When you enter text an auto complete list will appear.

- Under search outcomes, click on a student or a grouping.

- To invite more students or groups repeat steps four and five.

- Click Invite.

After emailing your invitation, the class list is updated so that they can name the invited students.

Inviting students by code

There are many ways to share the classroom code with your students. For example, you can display the code on a projector or copy and share it.

- Go to classroom.google.com.
- Click on Class.
- If you want the code to be displayed faster click **Full Screen**.
- Click **Settings** and select an option. To display the code on a projector, in the general section next to the code, click the down arrow.
- Instruct students to do the following: Go to classroom.google.com on the class page, click **Add** and then **Join**. Enter the code and tap the link.

Inviting students from other domains

If your IT administration has turned on the appropriate settings then you can invite students from outside your school domain.

Turn off, Reset, or Copy a class code

When you create a class the classroom automatically generates a class code. If the pupil has an issue with the class code, you can reset it. If you do not want new students to join your class you can also turn the code off. You can turn it back on at any time.

- Go to classroom.google.com.
- Clicking **Class** and then **Settings**.
- Under **General**, next to the class code, click the arrow and select an option:
  - To display the code, click **Display**.
  - To copy the code, click **Copy**.
  - To reset the code, click **Reset**.
  - To enable or disable the code, click **Disable** or **Enable**.
  - When you enable the code, the classroom generates a new class code.
- Click **Save**.

SETTING CLASSROOMS FOR STUDENTS

Like all Google apps, Google Classroom is accessible from any computer or mobile device connected to the Internet. However, not every student can access Google Classroom on the same device. Therefore, you must help and guide your students in joining and setting up classrooms. The best time to invite students to Google Classroom is at the beginning of a term. During the first day of class, advice your students on how to use the classroom, expectations, and familiarize your students with the curriculum and course syllabus. Setting up student devices to access online classes can easily integrate them into the process so they are ready to use Google Classroom as soon as possible and minimizes technical difficulties.

While the best time to set up Google Classroom with your students is the beginning of the term, this does not mean it should be the first day. Therefore, it may be more beneficial to wait until the majority of these changes are completed before inviting students to use Google Classroom. Doing this can save the number of manual changes you need to perform as you proceed. When students configure their devices or install software or apps for Google Classroom they prefer to use devices they use often. If your school already has a computer lab, mobile laptop, or Chromebook cart, students do not need to configure these devices. For a large number of students with personal laptops, tablets, or smart-phones, spending class time configuring their personal devices will increase their use of Google Classroom.

Google Classroom apps on iOS and Android provide push notifications. Encourage your students to install the app on their smartphone so they are always notified whenever an announcement or assignment is posted. You then don't have to worry about students checking emails sent by your school.

Because Google Classroom and other Apps require browsers, laptops running Microsoft Windows, Apple OS X, or Google's Chrome OS can already access Google Classroom. While Microsoft's default browser for Windows is Microsoft Edge, and Apple OS is Safari, Google develops and maintains its own Internet browser, Google Chrome. Using Chrome ensures the most excellent compatibility with Google Classroom. Chrome is already installed on Chromebooks so this device is the easiest to use while student profiles are automatically synced with this device when they first login with their school credentials, whether personal or a school-issued Chromebook. Chrome can be installed on Windows and OS X computers without administrator privileges, so even if students don't have an administrator account on the personal device they can still install the browser.

This option is if students want to sign in to the classroom to join.

CLASS CODES FOR STUDENTS

Using the classroom you will need to sign in to your PC or mobile and then join the class. After that, you can receive work from your tutors and talk to your classmates. Upon joining a class on one device you are enrolled in that class across all device. There are two ways to join the class:

Join the class with the class code: If your teacher gives you the class code use it to join the class. Your teacher can give you a code if you are in the class or they can email it to you.

Accept your teacher's invitation: If your teacher sends you an invitation you'll see a class code inserted on the classroom homepage. If you have deleted, lost, or forgotten the class code before joining, ask your teacher to resend it or have them set a new one.

If the code doesn't work, ask your teacher for help. You only need to use the class code once to join the class.

Connecting via computer

You must sign into the classroom before entering. Not sure if you're signing in? Learn more about signing up in the classroom.

Joining the class with the class code:

1. Go to classroom.google.com.

2. Be sure to sign in with the correct account. If you are already signed in and want to switch accounts you can do so in the upper right corner. Simply click your profile picture then select or add an account.

3. At the upper right-hand corner, select **Add** to join the class.

4. Enter the class code your tutor has given you and tap to join. A class code consists of 6 or 7 characters.

Accept your teacher's invitation:

1. Go to classroom.google.com.

2. Be sure to sign in with the correct account. If you are already signed in and want to switch accounts, you can do so in the upper right corner. Simply click your profile picture then select or add an account.

3. Click Join.

Connecting via Android

Join the class using the class code:

1. Click the classroom icon from Google applications.

2. Be sure to sign in with the correct account.

3. At the top tap Add-in and then join the class.

4. Enter the code your tutor gave you and tap to join. The class code consists of 6 or 7 characters.

Accept your teacher's invitation

1. Tap the classroom icon from Google application.

2. Be sure to sign in with the correct account.

3. On the class card tap **Join**.

Connecting via an iPhone or iPad

Join the class using the class code:

1. Tap on the classroom icon.

2. Be sure to sign in with the correct account.

3. In the bottom right corner tap **Add** and then join the class.

4. In the box enter the code your tutor gave you and tap **Join**. The code consists of 6 or 7 characters.

Accept your teacher's invitation:

1. Tap on the classroom icon from the Google application.

2. Be sure to sign in with the correct account.

3. On the card class, tap **Join**.

CHAPTER 03

CREATING ANNOUNCEMENTS

Now you have set up a classroom in Google Classroom and your students have entered their classes, you can start using the Classroom to interact with students. An easy way to communicate with pupils in your classroom is to post announcements. These announcements are like sending an email to your class. When you make an announcement, students also receive an email with the information. You can also add files from your computer or drive and add links to websites. Students can respond to your announcements directly from the classroom stream. Posts that appear in a stream can be used in questions and assignments. Using announcements instead of email is easier as you can find previous announcements and use them in other classes.

You can post announcements for your class on the Stream page and these do not have to have assignments attached to them. Posts are thoughts, queries, and information shared by students and teachers. You can add files, images, links, or videos, and comments are text-based replies to posts. Use these to communicate with your students. These announcements appear on the stream page in chronological order. Students receive an email for each announcement, but they can turn off email notifications if they prefer. You can use drafted announcements and can control who comments or responds to posts. The stream page has an option for students to post and comment; as a teacher, you can adjust their permission in Settings. Students cannot modify their posts or notes, but they can delete them. Only teachers can delete tasks and comments.

Creating announcements via a computer

New posts such as announcements, questions, or assignments are added to the top of the Stream. Old posts will move lower down the Stream.

You may post announcements to one or more modules or to selected pupils in the class. You can also add attachments.

1. Go to classroom.google.com.
2. Tap on the class.
3. On the Stream page, tap **share something with your class**.
4. Enter the announcement you want to make and click **Post**. As you type the announcement, the classroom automatically saves it and places a draft in saved announcements at the top of the Stream.

Posting an announcement to additional classes

If you want your announcement to post to multiple classes click the down arrow and then select the classes you want to post to.

Post to individual students

Unless you're posting in multiple classes, you can post announcements to individual students. You cannot post to more than 100 students at a time. Click **All students** and deselect this option. To select a student click on their name. On the Stream page, you can see the number of students who have announced the post. To view student names on the announcement, click the student number.

Adding attachments

You can add an attachment, such as Drive files, YouTube links, or links to your announcements. Google Drive items are only viewable (view-only) to students and are editable by co-teachers. To change these sharing options, see Stop, Limit, or Sharing. If you see a message stating you are not allowed to attach a file, click Copy. You can then attach this to the announcement and save it to the class drive folder.

Post, Schedule or Save draft announcements

As you type your announcement it will be automatically saved and a draft will be placed in the Saved Announcements section at the top of the Stream. If you see a message stating you are not allowed to add a file, click Copy. A copy will then be added to the classroom announcement section and it will be saved in the class drive. To post an announcement instantly, tap **Post**. To schedule the announcement, next to post click the down arrow and then click **Schedule**. Next to the date, tap the down arrow and choose the date and time you wish to post the announcement. To schedule the announcement for another class, first schedule it for one class and then again to another class. To save the announcement as a draft next to the post click on the down arrow and then **Save draft.** To view your planned and drafted posts, go to the top of the Stream page and select **Saved announcements**. To add a comment to a posted announcement select **Add class comment** under the post and select **Post**.

Editing Announcements

Edits affect individual classes. To edit announcements to more than one class you need to make an edit for each one.

For **posted** announcements:

On the stream page, next to the announcement, tap **More** (three vertical dots) and then **Edit**. Edit your post and click **Save**.

For a **planned** or **draft** announcement simply select the post. The announcement will appear and you can make your edits before selecting either **Post, Schedule** or **Save draft.**

REUSING POSTS

You can reuse announcements, assignments, or class questions. While reusing a post, you can:

- Use it in a real (physical) class or a different class.
- Make copies of attachments, including rubrics, or add new ones.
- Edit the post before publishing.

Note: You can reuse any assignment with rubrics on the web or mobile version of the class. For web only you can create, modify, or add rubrics.

Reusing posts via a computer

Note: If the post was originally sent to individual students, the post defaults to all students when you reuse it, but you can select individual students again if you wish. You cannot post to individual students through multiple classes. Many posts are shared with all students in the class.

If your reused post has a rubric you can edit the rubric in your new assignment. Your edits do not affect the rubric in the original assignment.

1. Go to classroom.google.com.

2. Tap on the class and select an option: To reuse any announcement on a stream page, click **Reuse post** for sharing something with your class. To reuse an assignment, question, or content, select **Classwork, Create** and then **Reuse post**.

3. Click on the class that contains the post you want to reuse.

4. Click on the post.

5. If you are copying the post to another class and you do not need to link the same attachment, **select Create new copies of all attachments**. It makes new documents in the drive folder of the class in which you are reusing the post.

6. Click **Reuse**.

7. Change information, add or remove any attachments.

8. Select:

    ▪ To save the post for later, next to consign, ask, or post, tap the down arrow and then **Save draft**.

    ▪ Click **Assign** if reusing an assignment.

    ▪ Click **Ask** if reusing a question.

    ▪ Click **Post** to reuse an announcement.

Reusing posts via Android

1. Tap the classroom.
2. Tap on the class and select an option:
   a. To reuse an announcement on a stream page, select share with your class and tap **Reuse post**.
   b. To reuse an assignment, question, or material, tap on classwork, and (+), then **Reuse post**.
3. Tap the class whose posts you want to reuse.
4. Tap on **Post**.
5. To create new copies of the original attachment, tap **Create**. Those copies can be found in the new class drive folder.
6. Make changes and add or remove any attachments. If the post has initially been sent to individual students when reusing the post will default to **All students**.
7. Select an option: **Post, Schedule, Save** or **Delete** a draft.

Reusing posts via iPhone or iPad

1. Tap the classroom.
2. Tap on the class and select an option:
   a. To reuse announcements on the stream page select share with your class and tap **Reuse post**.

    b. To reuse an assignment, question, or materials, tap on **Classwork** and add (+), and then **Reuse post**.

3. Tap the class whose posts you want to reuse.

4. Tap on **Post**.

5. To make or create new copies of all original attachments, tap **Create**. Those copies can be found in the new class drive folder.

6. Modify any information or add or remove any attachments. If this post has initially been sent to individual students it will default to **All students**, but you can re-select individual students if you wish. Select an option: **Post, Schedule** or **Delete** a draft.

Deleting an announcement:

1. Go to classroom.google.com.

2. Select an option:

    a. For posted announcements: On the stream page, next to the announcement, click more (three dots) and then **Delete**. To confirm, click **Delete** again.

    b. For scheduled or drafted announcements: At the top of the stream page click **Saved announcements**. Tap **Remove** (x) to delete.

You can move the announcement or any other post to the top of the stream.

1. Go to classroom.google.com.

2. Click on the class.

3. On the stream page, on the announcement click **More** (three dots option), and then **Move to top.**

MANAGING COMMENTS

Commenting on announcements:

Once these posts are published in the stream students and participating teachers can comment on the announcements. These comments encourage discussion and are akin to students asking questions after making a verbal announcement during class hours. Also, in other types of posts such as questions and assignments, students can use this commenting feature to answer specific questions within the post.

Replying to comments:

Individuals can reply to a specific comment on a post. Comments appear at the bottom of the commenting thread instead of directly below the comment that has been previously posted.

Post on the stream page (For Students)

If the teacher allows, students can interact with their class on the stream page using the posts, comments, and replies features.

What is the difference between post, comment and reply?

A post is an information or question you add to a class stream. For example: When do we go to the park?

Whereas **a comment** is a response or reply to a post or any other comments, for example: We go to park next Friday.

A reply is the answer or a response to someone's comment in which they are mentioned. For example: John is a commenter and he replies "Thanks!"

Note: Not all teachers allow posts and comments on the stream page.

If students do not want to post on the stream page they can send a personal comment to their assigned teacher on the assignment or question.

Creating a post

To ask a question or share information with teachers and classmates, create a post.

1. Go to classroom.google.com.
2. Click on the class.
3. Tap to share something with the class on the stream page.

If you do not see anything shared with the class or teacher then the teacher has turned off permissions to post.

Setting Student Permissions to Post and Comment

Students can post and comment on the stream page, or teachers can adjust their permission.

- Posts are opinions, queries, or information shared by students. They can be files, images, links, or videos.
- Comments are only text-based replies to posts.

Students cannot modify their posts or comments, but they can remove them. Teachers can remove any post or comment.

Controlling who can post to the stream page via a computer

1. Go to classroom.google.com.
2. Select the class and then **Settings**.

3. Near to **Stream**, under **General**, select **Students can post and comment** and then choose permission:

    a. **Students can post and comment**. This is the default option. Students can post on the stream page and comment on anything.

    b. **Students can only comment.** Students can comment on an existing post, but they cannot create a post.

    c. **Only teachers can post or comment**. Students cannot post or comment on the stream page. This option mutes all students.

4. In the top right corner, click **Save** to save your selection and return to the stream page.

Note: If you disable the right to post and comment on the stream page, students can still send private comments.

Controlling who can post to the stream page via Android

1. Click the classroom icon.
2. Click on the class and then **Settings**. You can only access the settings from the stream page
3. Under **General**, tap the stream settings and then choose permission:

a. **Students can post and comment.** This is the default option. Students can post on the stream page and comment on anything.

b. **Students can only comment.** Students can comment on an existing post, but they cannot create a post.

c. **Only teachers can post or comment.** Students cannot post or comment on the stream page. This option mutes all students.

4. To save your selection and exit settings, tap **Save** at the top.

Controlling who can post to the stream page via iPhone or iPad

1. Tap the classroom icon.
2. Tap on class and then **Settings**.
3. Under **Class settings**, tap **Stream Posting** and then choose permission:

a. **Students can post and comment.** This is the default option. Students can post on the stream page and comment on anything.

b. **Students can only comment.** Students can comment on an existing post, but they cannot create a post.

c. **Only teachers can post or comment**. Students cannot post or comment on the stream page. This option mutes all students.

4. Tap back to exit permissions and save.

5. Tap **Close** (x) to return to the stream page.

MUTING STUDENTS

If there is a student who is particularly inappropriate on the stream teachers can disable that student's ability to respond to comments on another classmate's work, post, or comments on the stream. In the stream and student list, a mute icon appears with the student's name so you can easily see which students are muted. Only teachers and co-teachers can see this icon.

Muting via a computer

Muting a student prevents them from posting or commenting on a particular class on the stream page. Students cannot see anything on the stream page to indicate they have been muted, they will just not be able to post. Students who are muted can still send personal comments. There are different ways to mute a student:

1. Go to classroom.google.com.

2. Tap on the class.

3. Tap the **People** icon.

4. Next to the student whom you want to mute, check the box.

5. Click **Actions**, and then click **Mute**.

6. To confirm, click **Mute** again.

Muting a student on their post or comment

1. Go to classroom.google.com.

2. Tap on the class.

3. Find the student post or comment.

4. Click **More** (three dots) and then mute the student's name.

5. To confirm, click **Mute**.

6. To delete a comment, click **More** (three dots) and then **Delete**. Click **Delete** again to confirm.

Muting via Android

1. Click the classroom icon.

2. Click the class, and then **People**.

3. Next to the name of the student, tap **More** (three dots) and then **Mute**.

4. To confirm tap **Mute** again.

Muting the student on their post or comment:

1. Click the classroom icon.

2. Click on the class.

3. Find post, comment, or reply.

4. Next to the student's name, tap **More** (three dots option) and then **Mute**.

5. To confirm tap **Mute** again.

Muting via iPhone or iPad

1. Click the classroom icon.

2. Click the class and then tap the **People** icon.

3. Tap the student's name.

4. In the upper right corner, click **More** (three dots) and then tap **Mute**.

5. Tap **Mute** again to confirm.

To mute a student on their post or comment:

1. Click the classroom icon.

2. Click on the class.

3. Find the student post or comment.

4. Next to the student's name, tap **More** (three dots) and then tap **Mute**.

5. To confirm tap **Mute** again.

CHAPTER 04

QUESTION & ANSWER SECTION

T he stream has many types of posts available and each type has a different set of features that permits teachers to interact with students in different ways. An example of this is when you want to have a conversation the same as you would in a physical classroom but through Google Classroom instead. There are many benefits to interacting with Google Classroom. In a generation of instant and text messaging, many students feel comfortable interacting with the platform online. Students do not have to be in one place to participate and they can take their time to respond. Therefore, students find these online discussions safer and they are less likely to fail.

CREATING QUESTIONS

Teachers can create short multiple-choice questions. After posting a question you can track the number of students responding to the stream page. You can also write questions for later use and post questions to individual students. Once students have submitted their work teachers can grade it and give it back to the students.

Creating questions via a computer

1. Go to classroom.google.com.

2. Select class and then **Classwork.**

3. At the top select **Create** and then click on **Question.**

4. Enter your question and any accompanying files.

5. For short questions, pupils can respond to each other and edit their answers. You can turn these options on or off.

   a. **Students can reply to each other** - select to permit students to view and comment on classmates' answers after they have answered the question.

   b. **Students can edit answer** – select to permit students to edit their response after submitting.

For posting to one or more classes:

Tap the down arrow and then choose the class or classes you want to join. You cannot post to individual students in multiple classes. By posting, many classes are shared with all pupils in classes.

Assigning to one or more students:

By default, a query is posted to all students in the class. You can post a query to individual students, however, if you add more than one class you cannot post to individual students. You cannot post to more than 100 individual students at a time.

1. Next to **All students**, click on the down arrow and then click **All students** to deselect it.

2. Select the students you want to view the question. On the stream page on the question, you can see the number of students asked. To see the names of the students click on the number of students on the question.

Adding a category:

You can add grades to the questions. With grade types, you and your pupils can see a category with a question, such as homework or an essay. Tutors also can see categories on the grade page.

Under **Grade category**, click the down arrow and then select a category from the menu.

Change points:

You can change points of a question or leave it ungraded. By default, questions are fixed at 100 points.

1. Tap the value under **Points**.

2. Enter a new value point or select **ungraded**. When students answer an ungraded question, they tap **Turn in**. If students miss their due date, the work

status shows missing or turned in late. Any work given without a due date shows as **Assigned.**

Creating multiple-choice questions:

1. Next to **Short answer**, tap the down arrow, and then click **Multiple choice.**

2. Tap on **Option 1** to enter your first answer choice.

3. Tap the **Add option** and select as many options as you like.

4. To delete an option click X.

5. By default, when students turn in a question they view a class review of the answers (replies). To turn off this feature, deselect **Students can see the class summary.**

Adding a due date & time:

By default, a question has no fixed date. To change it:

1. Tap the down arrow under **Due.**

2. Tap on a date on the calendar.

3. To set a due time, click time and then enter time and fix AM or PM.

   Note: Work is marked missing or turned in late until the date and time are fixed.

Adding a title or topic:

1. Under Topic, tap the down arrow.

2. Select a choice: **Create topic** and enter the topic name or select a topic from the list.

Adding attachments:

You can include content with your questions, such as Drive files, links, or YouTube clips. To upload a file, click **Attach**, choose the file and select the upload link.

To attach a Google Drive file:

1. Click **Drive**.

2. Choose an item and tap **Add**. If you see a message stating you are not allowed to attach a file, click **Copy**. The classroom makes a copy you can attach to the question and saves it in the Class Drive folder.

To attach a YouTube clip select YouTube and:

1. Look for a video to attach: In the search box, enter keywords and tap **search**. Click on the video and then add it.

2. To attach a video link: Click on the URL. Enter the URL and click **Add**. To attaching a link, click the link, enter the URL, and click **Add Link**. To delete an attachment select **Remove**.

Creating questions via Android

1. Tap on the classroom icon and then the class.
2. Tap **Classwork**.
3. Tap Add (+) and then tap **Question**.
4. Enter questions and directives.
5. For short answer questions, students can respond to each other and modify their answers. You can turn these options on or off.

    a. **Students can reply to each other** - select to permit students to view and comment on classmates' answers after they have answered the question.

    b. **Students can edit answer** – select to permit students to edit their response after submitting.

To post to one or more classes:

1. Next to the class label, tap **Next**.
2. Tap on any additional classes and then **Done**. You cannot post to individual students in multiple classes. Posts to many classes are shared with all students in the class.

Assigning to one or more students:

By default, questions are posted to all students in the class. You can post a question to individual students, however, if you add more than one class, you cannot post to individual students and you cannot post to more than 100 students at a time.

1. Tap **All students** and then again to change the selection.

2. Tap the student's name you want to see questions.

3. Tap **Done**. You can now see the number of students who are assigned questions in the class stream. To see student names tap the number of students on the question.

Adding a grade type:

You can add grades to the questions. With grade types, you and your pupils can see a category with a question, such as homework or an essay. Tutors also can see categories on the grade page.

You can assign categories to a mobile device, but you can only create new categories on one computer.

Under **Grade category**, click the down arrow and then select a category from the menu.

Change points:

You can change points of a question or leave it ungraded. By default, questions are fixed at 100 points.

1. Tap the value under Points.

2. Enter a new value point or select **ungraded**. When students answer an ungraded question, they tap **Turn in**. If students miss their due date, the work status shows missing or turned in late. Any work given without a due date shows as **Assigned**.

3. Tap **Save.**

Creating multiple-choice questions:

1. Next to **Short answer**, tap the down arrow, and then click **Multiple choice**.

2. Tap on **Option 1** to enter your first answer choice.

3. Tap the **Add option** and select as many options as you like.

4. To delete an option click X.

5. By default, when students turn in a question they view a class review of the answers (replies). To turn off this feature, deselect **Students can see the class summary.**

Adding a due date & time:

By default, there is no fixed date for questions. To change it:

1. Tap **no due date**, then **choose a date**, and then click **OK**.

2. To add a time type the time, enter and tap **OK**. Until a date or time are selected the work is marked missing or late.

Adding a topic:

1. Tap **No Topic**.

2. Select a choice: **Add topic** and enter the topic name or choose a topic from the list.

3. Tap **Save**.

Adding attachments:

You can include drive files, links, photos, or YouTube videos to your question.

1. For attaching, click **Attach** and select. If you see a message stating you are not allowed to attach a file, tap **Copy**. The classroom creates a copy to attach to the question and saves it in the Class Drive folder.

2. To add a drive item click the drive then select the item.

3. To attach a link, click the link enter the URL and click **Add**.

4. To attach a file from the current device click **File Upload**, then select the file and then **Open**.

5. To attach a YouTube video tap YouTube and select a choice. To search for a video file to attach type in the keywords in the search box and tap search. For attaching a video link enter the URL in the search box, tap the video and then tap to insert.

6. To take a photo and attach it click to take a photo from the camera and then tap done.

7. To record a video, tap to record a video then tap done.

8. For add a new PDF file, tap **new PDF.** When you're done, tap **More** (three dots) and then **Save.**

9. To delete an attachment tap **Delete** (X).

Creating questions via an iPhone or iPad

1. Tap the classroom and then tap the class.

2. Tap Classwork.

3. Add a question.

4. Enter your questions and directions.

5. For short answer questions, students can respond to one other and modify their answers. You can turn these options on or off.

   a. **Students can reply to each other** - select to permit students to view and comment on classmates' answers after they have answered the question.

b.   **Students can edit answer** – select to permit students to edit their response after submitting.

Posting to one or more classes:

1. Next to the class name, tap **Next**.
2. Select any added classes and tap **Done**. You cannot post to individual students in multiple classes. Multiple Posts are shared with all students in the class.

Assigning to one or more students:

By default, questions are posted to all students in the class. You can post a question to individual students, however, if you add more than one class, you cannot post to individual students and you cannot post to more than 100 students at a time.

1. Tap **All students** and then again to change the selection.
2. Tap the student's name you want to see questions.
3. Tap **Done**. You can now see the number of students who are assigned questions in the class stream. To see student names tap the number of students on the question.

Adding a grade type:

You can add grades to the questions. With grade types, you and your pupils can see a category with a question, such as homework or an essay. Tutors also can see categories on the grade page.

You can assign categories to a mobile device, but you can only create new categories on one computer.

Under **Grade category**, click the down arrow and then select a category from the menu.

Change points:

You can change points of a question or leave it ungraded. By default, questions are fixed at 100 points.

> 1. Tap the value under Points.
>
> 2. Enter a new value point or select **ungraded**. When students answer an ungraded question, they tap **Turn in**. If students miss their due date, the work status shows missing or turned in late. Any work given without a due date shows as **Assigned**.
>
> 3. Tap **Save**.

Creating multiple-choice questions:

> 1. Next to **Short answer**, tap the down arrow, and then click **Multiple choice**.
>
> 2. Tap on **Option 1** to enter your first answer choice.

3. Tap the **Add option** and select as many options as you like.

4. To delete an option click X.

5. By default, when students turn in a question they view a class review of the answers (replies). To turn off this feature, deselect **Students can see the class summary.**

Adding a due date & time:

By default, there is no fixed date for questions. To change it:

3. Tap **no due date**, then **choose a date**, and then click **OK**.

4. To add a time type the time, enter and tap **OK**. Until a date or time are selected the work is marked missing or late.

Adding a topic:

4. Tap **No Topic.**

5. Select a choice: **Add topic** and enter the topic name or choose a topic from the list.

6. Tap **Save.**

Adding attachments:

You can include drive files, links, photos, or YouTube videos to your question.

1. For attaching, click **Attach** and select. If you see a message stating you are not allowed to attach a

file, tap **Copy**. The classroom creates a copy to attach to the question and saves it in the Class Drive folder.

2. To attach a link, click the link enter the URL and click **Add**.

3. To attach a file from the current device click **File Upload**, then select the file.

4. For attaching an image, tap to select the photo.

5. For taking a picture, tap to use the camera. Take a picture and then tap **Use photo**.

6. To delete an attachment tap **Remove** (X).

MANAGING STUDENT RESPONSES

(For Students)

Answers or multiple-choice questions are posted by teachers. After posting a questions teachers can track the number of student replies on the stream page. Teachers can also draft questions for later posting and post questions to individual students. When teachers ask or create a question they can instruct students to leave comments. In both multiple choice and short answer questions, students can read and answer class comments. Students can also make confidential comments to teachers. For short answer questions, students can respond to

Posting on the stream page

If the teacher permits, students can correspond with the class on the stream page using posts, comments and replies. A post is information or a question you add to a stream. A comment is a response to a post or other comment. Replies are responses to someone's comment in which they are mentioned. If you do not want to post on the stream page, you can send a personal comment on the assignment or on the questions asked.

each other and edit their own answers. Teachers can turn these options on or off.

Students can reply to each other. Select to permit students to view and comment on classmates' answers after they have answered the question.

Students can edit answer. Select for students to edit their response.

Posting via a computer

Creating a post:

To ask a question or share information with teachers and classmates, you need to create a post.

1. Go to classroom.google.com.
2. Click on the class.
3. Click to share something with the class on the stream page. If you do not see anything shared with your class then the teacher has turned off permissions for students to post.
4. Enter what you want to say and click on **Post**.

Adding a picture, file, video or link to your post:

Students can attach items to posts such as images, files, items from Google Drive, videos from YouTube, or links.

1. Follow the steps that are mentioned above to create a post.

2. Attach items to your post.

3. Click on the post. If you see a message stating you are not allowed to attach a file, click **Copy**. The classroom creates a copy, attaches it to your post and saves it in the Class Drive folder.

Delete a post:

You can only delete your posts. If you delete your post, all related comments associated with it are also deleted. You cannot undo this. Only teachers can delete someone's post and view all deleted posts.

1. Go to classroom.google.com.

2. Tap on the class.

3. On the post, tap **More** (three dots) and then **Delete**.

4. Tap **Delete** to confirm.

Adding a comment to a post:

If your teacher permits, you can comment on other posts and comments. Teachers can only delete comments and can turn off permissions to comment. Comments are text-only - you cannot add images, links, or videos.

1. Go to classroom.google.com.

2. Click on the class.

3. Find a post and add your comment. If you do not see **Add class comment**, your teacher has already turned off permissions to comment.

4. Click **Post**.

Replying to a comment:

When you reply to a comment, the person you are replying to is automatically mentioned. You can only use replies with comments, not posts.

1. Go to classroom.google.com.

2. Click on the class.

3. Find the comment and then click **Reply**. The person you are replying to is mentioned automatically in your reply.

4. Enter your reply and click on **Post**.

Deleting a comment:

You are only allowed to delete your own comments.

1. Go to classroom.google.com.

2. Click on the class.

3. On comments, tap **More** (three dots) and then **Delete**.

4. Click **Delete** again to confirm.

Sending a personal comment to your teacher:

You can leave comments to your teacher only they can see. When you are given work you can send personal comments to your teachers through the assignment or question platform.

1. Go to classroom.google.com.
2. Tap on the class.
3. Tap **Assignment** or **Question** on the stream page.
4. To view the assignment or question, click **View assignment** or **View question**.
5. Add a private comment by selecting **Add a private comment.** Enter your comment and then click **Post.**

Posting via Android

Creating a post:

1. Tap the classroom.
2. Tap on the class.
3. Click to share something with the class on the stream page. If you do not see anything shared with your class then the teacher has turned off permissions for students to post.
4. Enter what you want to say and click on **Post.**

Adding a picture, file, video or link to your post:

Students can attach items to posts such as images, files, items from Google Drive, videos from YouTube, or links.

1. Follow the steps that are mentioned above to create a post.

2. Attach items to your post.

3. Click on the post. If you see a message stating you are not allowed to attach a file, click **Copy**. The classroom creates a copy, attaches it to your post and saves it in the Class Drive folder.

Delete a post:

You can only delete your posts. If you delete your post, all related comments associated with it are also deleted. You cannot undo this. Only teachers can delete someone's post and view all deleted posts.

1. Tap the classroom.

2. Tap on the class.

3. On the post, tap **More** (three dots) and then **Delete**.

4. Tap **Delete** to confirm.

Adding a comment to a post:

If your teacher permits, you can comment on other posts and comments. Teachers can only delete comments and can turn off permissions to comment. Comments are text-only - you cannot add images, links, or videos.

1. Tap the classroom.
2. Tap on the class.
3. On the post, tap Up and add a class comment.
4. Enter your comment and tap **Post**.

Deleting a comment:

You are only allowed to delete your own comments.

1. Tap the classroom.
2. Tap on the class.
3. Find the post with your comments and tap on the number next to class comments.
4. Tap Up on the comments and then **Delete**.
5. Tap **Delete** to confirm.

Sending a personal comment to your teacher:

You can leave comments to your teacher that only he or she can see. When you are given work, you can send personal comments to your teachers by using an assignment or question platform.

1. Tap the classroom.
2. Tap on the class.
3. On the stream page, tap on the question or assignment.

4. Tap on **Add a personal comment** then enter your comments and tap **Post**.

Posting via an iPhone or iPad

Creating a post:

1. Tap the classroom.
2. Tap on the class.
3. Click to share something with the class on the stream page. If you do not see anything shared with your class then the teacher has turned off permissions for students to post.
4. Enter what you want to say and click on **Post**.

Adding a picture, file, video or link to your post:

Students can attach items to posts such as images, files, items from Google Drive, videos from YouTube, or links.

1. Tap in the classroom.
2. Tap on the class.
3. On the stream page, tap on **Share with your class**. If you do not see anything shared with your class then the teacher has turned off permissions for students to post.
4. Attach the attachments.
5. Add a message to the post - you cannot post an attachment without a message.

6. Tap on **Post**. If you see a message stating you are not allowed to attach a file tap **Copy**.

Delete a post:

You can only delete your posts. If you delete your post, all related comments associated with it are also deleted. You cannot undo this. Only teachers can delete someone's post and view all deleted posts.

1. Tap the classroom.
2. Tap on the class.
3. On the post, tap **More** (three dots) and then **Delete**.
4. Tap **Delete** to confirm.

Adding a comment to a post:

If your teacher permits, you can comment on other posts and comments. Teachers can only delete comments and can turn off permissions to comment. Comments are text-only - you cannot add images, links, or videos.

1. Tap the classroom.
2. Tap on the class.
3. On the post, tap Up and add a class comment.
4. Enter your comment and tap **Post**.

Deleting a comment:

You are only allowed to delete your own comments.

1. Tap the classroom.

2. Tap on the class.

3. Find the post with your comments and tap on the number next to class comments.

4. Tap Up on the comments and then **Delete**.

5. Tap **Delete** to confirm.

Sending a personal comment to your teacher:

You can leave comments to your teacher that only he or she can see. When you are given work, you can send personal comments to your teachers by using an assignment or question platform.

1. Tap the classroom.

2. Tap on the class.

3. On the stream page, tap on the question or assignment.

4. Tap on **Add a personal comment** then enter your comments and tap **Post**.

CHAPTER 05

ASSIGNMENTS

When you create an assignment you can post it right away, save as a draft, or schedule it for posting at a later date. Once students have started work and handed over their assignments, teachers can grade and return them to students. The three device options Google provides are computers, Android systems, and iOS (iPhones and iPads).

CREATING AND POSTING ASSIGNMENTS

When you create an assignment you can post it to one or more classes. When posting to individual students you can add a grading category, change the point value, add a due date or time, add a topic, add attachments and turn on originality reports.

Creating an assignment via a computer:

1. Go to classroom.google.com.

2. Click on the class and then click **Classwork**.

3. At the top of the page, click **Create** and then click **Assignment**.

4. Enter the title and instructions.

Posting to one or more classes:

Under **For**, click the down arrow and then choose the class or classes you want to add. You cannot post to individual students in multiple classes. Posts shared with many classes are shared with all students in all classes.

Post to individual students:

By default, assignments are posted to all students in the class. You can post the assignment to an individual student, however, if you add more than one class you cannot post to an individual student and you cannot post to more than 100 students at a time.

1. Next to **All students**, click on the down arrow and then deselect All students.

2. Select the students whom you want to post the assignments to.

Add a category:

You can include grading categories for assignments where teachers and students can view categories related to the assignment, such as homework or essays. Teachers can also see categories on the grade page. Under **Grade Category**, click the down arrow and then select a category from the menu.

Changing the point value:

You can change the point value of assignments or leave it ungraded. By default, the assignment is fixed at 100 points.

1. Click the value under **Points**.
2. Enter a new value point or select **Ungraded**. Students completing an ungraded assignment can tap to turn in or if no file is turned in they mark it as done. If the student does not turn in or mark as done before the specified date the assignment is marked as missing. If no due date is given it is marked as assigned.

Adding a due date or time:

By default, no assignment has a due date. To change it:

1. Under **Due** next to **No due date**, click the down arrow.
2. Click on the date which will show you the calendar.
3. Set a due time by clicking the time and then enter the time specifying AM or PM. Work can be marked **Missing** or **Turned in late** as soon as the date and time have been selected.

Adding a topic:

1. Click the down arrow under **Topic**.

2. Select an option: **Create topic** and enter the topic name or select the topic from the list. You can only add one topic to the assignment.

Adding attachments:

You can add attachments to assignments using files from your computer, Google Drive, videos from YouTube, or links.

To delete an attachment click **Remove** (X). To decide how students interact with the attachment, click the down arrow below the attachment and then select an option:

1. **Students can view the file**. All students can read the file but cannot edit it.

2. **Students can edit the file**. If all students are sharing the same file they can make changes to it.

3. **Make a copy for each student.** Students can get a copy of their file with their name added to the title of the document. For Google Docs, Sheets, and Slide files, both teachers and students can edit the document. When students hand over the assignments, they cannot edit the document unless you return it to them. If you see a message stating you are not allowed to attach a file, click

Copy. The classroom creates a copy, attaches it to the classroom assignment and saves it in the Class Drive folder.

Posting, scheduling, or saving a draft assignment:

When you create an assignment, you can post it right away, schedule it to post later or save it as a draft. Click **Classwork** to view scheduled and drafted assignments. Click the assigned link to post the assignment quickly.

Scheduling the assignment to be posted later:

1. Click the down arrow and then select **Schedule**.
2. Click the down arrow next to the date and select the time and date. The time defaults to PM until you change it to AM
3. Click **Schedule**. Assignments are posted automatically on the scheduled date and time. To schedule the assignment for another class, first schedule an assignment for another class, schedule it and then reuse the assignment for another class.
4. To submit, click on the arrow and then **Save draft.**

Creating an assignment via Android

Create an assignment:

1. Tap the classroom and then class.

2. Tap on **Classwork**.

3. Tap on **Add** (+) and then tap the assignment.

4. Enter the title and instructions.

Post to one or more classes:

1. Next to the class name, tap **Next**.

2. Tap on any additional classes and then select Done. You cannot post to individual students in multiple classes. All posts to multiple classes are shared with all students in the class.

Post to individual students:

By default, assignments are posted to all students in the class. You can post the assignment to an individual student, however, if you add more than one class you cannot post to an individual student and you cannot post to more than 100 students at a time.

1. Tap **All students** and then again to deselect it.

2. Select the students you want to post assignments to.

3. Tap **Done**.

Add a category:

You can include grading categories for assignments where teachers and students can view categories related to the assignment, such as homework or essays. Teachers can also see categories on the grade page.

You can add a category to an assignment on mobile, but you can only create categories on a computer.

1. Next to grading tap **No category.**
2. Select the category.
3. Create assignments or tap **More** (three dots) and then **Save draft.**

Changing the point value:

You can change the point value of assignments or leave it ungraded. By default, the assignment is fixed at 100 points.

1. Click the value under **Points.**
2. Enter a new value point or select **Ungraded.** Students completing an ungraded assignment can tap to turn in or if no file is turned in they mark it as done. If the student does not turn in or mark as done before the specified date the assignment is marked as missing. If no due date is given it is marked as assigned.

Adding a due date or time:

By default, assignments have no due date. To change it:

1. Tap **No due date**, select a date and then tap **OK**.

2. Select a time and then tap **OK**. As soon as timing and date of the assignment are set then assignments can be marked as **Missing** or **Turned in late**.

Adding a title or topic:

1. Tap **No Topic**.

2. Select an option: **Create topic** and enter the title name or select the title or topic from the list.

3. Tap **Save**. You can only add one topic to an assignment.

Adding attachments:

For attaching files select **Attach** and then select an option. If you see a message stating you are not allowed to attach a file tap **Copy**. A copy is created and saved in the Class Drive folder.

To decide how students interact with the attachment tap Up next to the attachment and select an option:

1. **Students can view the file**. All students can read the file but cannot edit it.

2. **Students can edit the file**. If all students are sharing the same file they can make changes to it.

3. **Make a copy for each student.** Students can get a copy of their file with their name added to the title of the document. For Google Docs, Sheets, and Slide files, both teachers and students can edit the document. When students hand over the assignments, they cannot edit the document unless you return it to them. To delete an attachment tap the preview and then tap **Delete.**

Posting, scheduling, or saving a draft assignment:

When you create an assignment, you can post it right away, schedule it to post later or save it as a draft. Click **Classwork** to view scheduled and drafted assignments. Click the assigned link to post the assignment quickly.

Scheduling the assignment to be posted later:

1. Tap **More** (three dots) and then **Schedule.**
2. Select a date and time.
3. Tap **Schedule.** Assignments are posted automatically on the scheduled date and time. To schedule assignments in another class first schedule it for one class and then select **Reuse Post** for another class.

For saving the assignment as a draft, tap **More** (three dots) and then **Save draft.**

Creating an assignment via iPhone or iPad

Create an assignment:

1. Tap the classroom and then class.

2. Tap on **Classwork.**

3. Tap on **Add** (+) and then tap the assignment.

4. Enter the title and instructions.

Post to one or more classes:

1. Next to the class name, tap **Next.**

2. Tap on any additional classes and then select **Done.** You cannot post to individual students in multiple classes. All posts to multiple classes are shared with all students in the class.

Post to individual students:

By default, assignments are posted to all students in the class. You can post the assignment to an individual student, however, if you add more than one class you cannot post to an individual student and you cannot post to more than 100 students at a time.

1. Tap **All students** and then again to deselect it.

2. Select the students you want to post assignments to.

3. Tap **Done.**

Add a category:

You can include grading categories for assignments where teachers and students can view categories related to the assignment, such as homework or essays. Teachers can also see categories on the grade page.

You can add a category to an assignment on mobile, but you can only create categories on a computer.

1. Next to grading tap **No category**.
2. Select the category.
3. Create assignments or tap **More** (three dots) and then **Save draft**.

Changing the point value:

You can change the point value of assignments or leave it ungraded. By default, the assignment is fixed at 100 points.

1. Click the value under **Points**.
2. Enter a new value point or select **Ungraded** then tap **Save**. Students completing an ungraded assignment can tap to turn in or if no file is turned in they mark it as done. If the student does not turn in or mark as done before the specified date the assignment is marked as missing. If no due date is given it is marked as assigned.

Adding a due date or time:

By default, no assignment has a due date. To change it:

1. Tap **No due date**, select a date and then tap **OK**.

2. Select a time and then tap **OK**.

Adding a title or topic:

1. Tap **No Topic**.
2. Select an option: **Create topic** and enter the title name or select the title or topic from the list.
3. Tap **Save**. You can only add one topic to an assignment.

Adding attachments:

For attaching files select **Attach** and then select an option. If you see a message stating you are not allowed to attach a file tap **Copy**. A copy is created and saved in the Class Drive folder.

To decide how students interact with the attachment tap Up next to the attachment and select an option:

1. **Students can view the file**. All students can read the file but cannot edit it.
2. **Students can edit the file**. If all students are sharing the same file they can make changes to it.

Posting, scheduling, or saving a draft assignment:

When you create an assignment, you can post it right away, schedule it to post later or save it as a draft. Click **Classwork** to view scheduled and drafted assignments. Click the assigned link to post the assignment quickly.

Scheduling the assignment to be posted later:

1. Tap **More** (three dots) and then **Schedule**.

2. Select a date and time.

3. Tap **Schedule**. Assignments are posted automatically on the scheduled date and time. To schedule assignments in another class first schedule it for one class and then select **Reuse Post** for another class.

STUDENT FILES (ASSIGNMENTS & GRADING)

Google Classroom works with Google Doc files, stored files in Google Drive, and Gmail so teachers can assign tasks to students. Teachers can link document files, websites, and photos to assignments using Google's various software and applications. All activities conducted are online using either a computer or mobile device. Teachers can plan assignments and use this option for when students see assignments and related attachments. Teachers can observe students when they carry out activities such as seeing their upcoming work, completing it online, and turning in their work to the teacher.

The teacher can post to more than one class or individual students in one or more classes and set specific due dates. Teachers may access and control any file until a date and time are specified.

When a Drive file (Docs, Slides, or Sheets) is attached teachers can choose:

1. **Students can view the file.** Students can read the files but cannot edit them.

2. **Students can edit the file.** The same file is shared by students and they can edit it.

3. **Make a copy for each student.** Students can get an individual copy of the file they can edit. The student's name is added automatically to the title of the document file. When a student hands back the assignment after editing, the teacher views the file with the name of the student. When working on the assignment the teacher can see student progress and can add comments and edit the file.

While working on their assignments either by viewing the file or editing or changing their copy students can attach files, images, or photos to their assignment. Upon completion, they can submit or turn in their work to the teacher.

If the due date or assigned date is available, then before that date the student can obtain their files, modify them, and resubmit. After submission, only the teacher can modify or edit the file.

Grading

Google Classroom facilitates teachers in providing numerical grades and commenting (feedback). If the teacher deems it necessary they can return the assignment without a grade.

The teacher can give grades and return work using the classroom grading tool and the grades page.

Grading via a computer

To see student assignments and even before seeing student assignments teachers can see student work status and the number of students in each category.

1. Go to classroom.google.com.

2. Click on the class.

3. At the top click **Classwork, Assignments** and then **View assignments.**

4. On the student work page, you can see the number and name of students grouped by their assignment status.

   Assigned Status means students have to submit work, including missing or non-submitted work.

   Turned in or Submitted status - when students submit their work.

   Graded Status where submitted work is graded.

   Returned Status Not graded (ungraded) work you have returned.

For importing grades make sure Quiz is the only attachment. You can edit the assignment until you have turned on the grading import option. (Importing the quiz option is available via a computer only).

1. Go to classroom.google.com.

2. Click on the class.

3. At the top click **Classwork**, **Assignments** and then **View assignments**.

4. In the upper right, click **Import Grade**.

5. Click **Import** to confirm.

6. To return grades to each student check the box of the student and then click the return option. Students can then view their grades in the classrooms and forms.

Grading via Android, iPhone and iPad

To see student assignments and even before seeing student assignments teachers can see student work status and the number of students in each category.

1. Tap in the classroom.

2. Tap on the class and then **Classwork** and then **Assignment**.

3. You can see the status of the student's work on the student work page.

   Assigned Status means students have to submit work, including missing or non-submitted work.

   Turned in or Submitted Status - when students submit their work.

   Graded Status where submitted work is graded.

Returned Status Not graded (ungraded) work you have returned

4. To view student-submitted work just tap their name and see the files they have attached.

Editing and reviewing grades

When you give grades to students by entering them, they sync between the grading page, the grading tool, and the student's work page. As a teacher, when you grade, the work, assignment or grade status is color-coded. **Red** means missing work. **Green** means turned in or the grade is drafted. **Black** means work is returned. Other colors do not indicate a work or grade status.

Editing and reviewing grades via a computer

When you want to enter grades on the work page of student:

1. Go to classroom.google.com.
2. Click on the class.
3. At the top select **Classwork, Assignments** and then **View Assignments**.
4. Click on the thumbnail to open and review any file associated with the student.
5. The default point value is 100. To change it, click **Point Value**. Enter a different value or select **Ungraded** and then update.

6. Next to student name enter the grade.

7. For any other student, enter their grades.

Students get a grade upon receiving the returned assignment.

Entering grades in the rating tool:

Use a grading tool to give personalized feedback. The default grade denominator is 100, but it can be changed to any number greater than zero. Changes in grade denominator only affect assignments not returned. Returned assignments maintain your original denominator.

1. Open student assignments in the grading tool.

2. Click on **Grading**.

3. Enter the grade under **Grade**.

Viewing assignment grades and submission dates:

You can see how the grade for the assignment has changed and how many times a student has submitted the assignment.

1. Go to classwork.google.com.

2. At the top click **Classwork, Assignments** and then **View assignments**.

3. On the left, click on a student's name.

4. Click **View history**.

Changing the grade:

You can change grades after returning assignments to students.

1. Go to classroom.google.com.

2. Click on the class.

3. At the top, click **Classwork, Assignments** and then **View assignments.**

4. Next to the name of the student, click the grade you want to change.

5. Enter a new number. The new grade is saved automatically.

6. Click **Return** and then again to confirm.

Editing and reviewing grades via Android, iPhone and iPad

As a teacher you can enter grades on the student page:

You can edit or comment on any document file in the drive. When the student opens the document file the edits or comments you have made are automatically saved. You can also add feedback directly to student work.

1. Tap in the classroom.

2. Tap on class and then **Classwork** and **Assignment.**

3. The default point value is 100. To change it, tap on the point value at the top. Enter another value to change it.

4. Tap in the name of the student.

5. Tap to add grades and then tap **Done**.

6. Choose: Tap back for the student work page or tap up to return.

Viewing assignment grades and the submission dates:

You can see grade changes for assignments and the number of times a student has submitted the assignment.

1. Tap in the classroom.

2. Tap on class and then **Classwork** and **Assignment**.

3. Tap in the name of the student.

4. At the top, tap **More** (three dots) and then **View history**.

Changing the grade:

You can change grades after returning assignments to students. Students can also carry out more work and reschedule to submit assignments. You can then change the grade to the returned assignment.

1. Tap in the classroom.

2. Tap on the class and then **Classwork** and **Assignment**.

3. Tap in the student name whose grades you want to change.

4. Tap to add the grade and then tap **Done**.

5. Choose: Tap back for the student work page or tap up to return.

CHAPTER 06

TIPS AND TRICKS

G oogle Classroom permits teachers to provide grades on assignments, interact with students, create templates for tasks, and more. Most teachers now work from home which is the perfect time to master Google Classroom and assign students the responsibility to continue their education during lockdown due to the current global outbreak.

A FEW TIPS AND TRICKS

Below are a few helpful tips and tricks for teachers. These increase the possibility of learning more and make Google Classroom more effective.

1. **Changing themes:**

When creating a new class, teachers can include details such as names, descriptions, and images to create a unique online classroom environment. Teachers can choose from s default theme group or upload photos from their computer. Grouped themes are simple to use as they are divided into subjects. Tap on the selected theme in the title icon, select the theme and apply it to the classroom. Copy the class code and invite students to join the class.

2. Change folder color:

A fundamental rule essential for when teachers are managing dozens of classes and subjects at a time. By default, all created classes are saved in the Google Drive folder. You can easily change the class folder color for easy search and unique personalization. Go to class, **Classwork** then **Class Drive folder** to open the corresponding folder on Google Drive. You can also rename it and add numbers to the title. Then, to set the color of the new folder, right-click and select **Change Color** from the menu.

3. Educational responsibilities:

Teachers have a responsibility to use and promote the program. It is a must-have for any affiliate. Google Classroom has already added the ability to set new standards. Teachers can create an assignment, add details, comments, grading, or publish or schedule posts for a specific time.

4. Integrating Google Calendar:

Google Classroom creates a separate calendar for each class in Google Calendar. Go to class, **Classwork** and select **Google Calendar**. Here you can find different calendars for the classes you have created. If you do not want it to interfere with your own calendar, remove your name. Users can also change calendar color.

5. Referencing content:

When assigning tasks it's beneficial to provide source material for the project. Go to **Teachers**, **Content Creation** and add title, description, and source documents from Google Docs, Forms, YouTube, or the Internet, then select the category and tap **Publish**.

6. Using personal comments:

Teachers can assign total grade points to tasks. After students submit work teachers can rate it. What's more, teachers can use the private comment function to complement students personally.

7. Students who sort by name and first name:

It's hard to focus on grades when dealing with hundreds of students in the classroom. When grading takes place, teachers can sort students by a nickname or first name using the filter menu. This makes the whole grading process easier.

8. Sending email:

Google Classroom permits teachers to send email to all students on the go. Teachers can always email students individually but this is more cumbersome. Emails can be sent from the classroom interface. To do this, can go to **Marks**, select **Assignment, All students** from the drop-down menu, and then select the student's email.

9. Inviting teachers:

Google Classroom allows you to invite other teachers into the classroom during class. When in the classroom, go to **People** and tap the share button to invite other teachers into the classroom.

10. Communicating internally:

Teachers can use this function to initiate discussion among students. Go to Class, **Classwork, Create** and then **Question**. You can add a question and choose between short answers or multiple options, add instructions, attach files and, most importantly, enable students to post questions from the sidebar. You can also allow students to add feedback on this topic internally.